Steven
SPIELBERG

Steven SPIELBERG

by D. L. Mabery

Lerner Publications Company
Minneapolis

LIBRARY OF CONGRESS CATALOGING-IN-PUBLICATION DATA

Mabery, D.L.
Steven Spielberg.

Summary: A biography of a young movie producer, director, and writer who, as a personal mission, helps other young movie-makers get their start.
1. Spielberg, Steven, 1947-   — Juvenile literature. 2. Moving-picture producers and directors — United States — Biography — Juvenile literature. [1. Spielberg, Steven, 1947-
2. Motion Picture producers and directors] I. Title.
PN1998.A3S6842   1986   791.43′0233′0924   [B]   [92]   86-10305
ISBN 0-8225-1612-8 (lib. bdg.)

1 2 3 4 5 6 7 8 9 10 96 95 94 93 92 91 90 89 88 87 86

Contents

When Dreamers Dream

Steven Spielberg is a dreamer. He has a vivid imagination, and he is constantly dreaming up characters and stories. His imagination is so active that a friend of his has said that Steven Spielberg has a new idea every thirteen seconds. Many people are dreamers, but what sets Steven Spielberg apart from most everybody else who is fond of daydreaming is that Steven's dreams can be brought to life. Or, more correctly, his dreams can be made into movies.

Steven Spielberg is, of course, a movie director. He is

the most successful movie director of the 1970's and 1980's, and will quite possibly be known some day as the most successful movie director of all time. His movies have been viewed by millions of people not only in his native United States, but in every major nation in the world. His pictures regularly break box office records. For instance, *Jaws*, released in 1975, made more money than any movie before it in the history of Hollywood.

The record that *Jaws* set, however, has since been broken—and it was broken by a movie Steven made. In 1982, Steven released a movie about a creature from outer space. The creature is left behind on Earth when the spaceship it was traveling on leaves Earth very quickly. The creature meets a shy and lonely boy, and the two become best friends. That movie was *E.T.: The Extra-Terrestrial*. By 1986, *E.T.* still held the record for making more money than any movie ever. People loved the heartwarming story so much that they went to see the movie over and over.

Most of Spielberg's movies have enjoyed similar success. In a 1986 list of the top twenty most popular movies, five were made by Steven Spielberg. *E.T.*, as we've noted, is in first place. *Jaws* is number five, *Raiders of the Lost Ark* is number seven, *Indiana Jones and the Temple of Doom* is number eight, and *Close Encounters of the Third Kind* is number fifteen. One other movie in the top twenty, *Gremlins* (number seventeen), was conceived and developed by Steven, although he did not direct it.

Although Steven has enjoyed success as a movie director, he did not grow up with everything handed to him on a silver platter. In fact, Steven's childhood was rather ordinary—except for the fact that he liked to make movies. And a lot of the ordinary things he did while growing up have inspired scenes in the movies he later made.

TAKE ONE: Back to His Childhood

Arnold Spielberg, Steven's father, worked in the computer industry. In the late 1940's and early 1950's, computer technology was quite new. Arnold knew that someday computers would greatly benefit the human race. Computers could help us reach the moon, and could become a tool to improve education.

Arnold's wife, Leah, was his opposite. She loved classical music and knew very little about scientific research. Leah played the piano and performed with a small chamber orchestra.

Mr. and Mrs. Spielberg were living in Cincinnati, Ohio, when Steven was born on December 18, 1947. While Steven was still a baby, his father bought a movie camera to take pictures of his <u>son</u>. Mrs. Spielberg watched in amazement as the child instinctively knew what to do. "He got up and walked straight for the camera," she recalled years later.

Steven's mother encouraged him to be as creative as he wanted to be. Steven still loves classical music, but with the exception of the clarinet, he never really played any musical instrument. His fondness for music is the reason most of his movies have very dramatic musical scores.

Steven's parents, Leah and Arnold, and his wife-to-be, Amy Irving, went to the annual Screen Directors Guild Awards dinner with him in 1976.

While Mrs. Spielberg was encouraging Steven's creative side, Mr. Spielberg was introducing him to science. When Steven was only six years old, Arnold woke the boy at two o'clock in the morning and drove him out to a meadow to watch a meteor shower. It was the first time Steven had really paid attention to the sky, and it filled him with a sense of wonder. Years later, he shared that wonder with movie audiences in *Close Encounters of the Third Kind*. This movie is about space beings who make contact with a group of Earth's scientists. The aliens' spaceship descends dramatically from the night sky, and the audience feels the same wonder Steven did when he was looking at the sky at the age of six.

Steven did not share all of his father's enthusiasm for computer technology. Occasionally he made fun of his father's work. When Steven was about eleven years old, Mr. Spielberg brought home a tiny transistor, an electronic device used in the transmission of radio and television signals.

Mr. Spielberg gathered his family around the kitchen table. "This is the future," he said. Steven picked up the transistor and put it in his mouth—and swallowed it. At first his father laughed, thinking that Steven was pretending to have eaten the chip. When he realized that Steven wasn't faking, that he had swallowed it, Mr. Spielberg was not pleased.

Arnold Spielberg's job as a computer engineer meant he had to move his family around the country to wherever work was available. When Steven was only four years old, the Spielbergs moved from Cincinnati to Haddenfield, New Jersey. When he was nine, the family moved again, this time to Scottsdale, Arizona, a suburb of Phoenix. And when Steven was sixteen, they moved to Saratoga, on the outskirts of San Jose, California. Steven has always considered Arizona to be home, however, because of the years he spent growing up and going to high school there.

Jumping from city to city naturally had an effect on the future movie director. "Just as I'd become accustomed to a school and a teacher and a best friend, the 'For Sale' sign would dig into the front lawn and we'd be packing and off to some other state," Steven remembers. Moving made it tough for him to maintain long-lasting friendships. For that reason, he began to develop a world of his own in his creative imagination.

As a child, Steven spent a lot of time by himself, and his own room was his favorite place to play. His room was always a mess. "My bedroom was like all the rooms of all the kids in all the movies I've been a part of," Steven has said. It never occurred to him to put anything away, so his jeans and shirt would land in a heap next to his model trains and comic books.

His bedroom not only held clothing and toys, but Steven's pets as well. When he was around ten or eleven, he got his first pets, some parakeets. Steven's parents decided parakeets would be easy pets to care for. Unlike a dog or a cat, parakeets wouldn't run around the house, and they would be easy to feed. However, Steven let the birds roam free in his bedroom, and trained them

Maybe the reason Steven directs movies about children is that he never really grew up. He knows how to explain what he wants to Henry Thomas ("Elliott") on the set of *E.T.*

to live on the curtain rod over his window. At one time he had four parakeets living in his bedroom, and birdseed all over the floor.

Keeping the bedroom messy, and allowing the birds to fly freely in it, kept the rest of the family out. Mrs. Spielberg now jokes that she would only stick her hand inside the door to get Steven's dirty clothes when she was doing laundry.

Steven has three sisters, all younger than he is—Ann, Sue, and Nancy. Being the oldest, and the only boy in the family, Steven was often left in charge of his sisters. That didn't please the girls, because quite often Steven would unleash his mischievous imagination on them.

Once Steven hid outside his sisters' bedroom window and pretended he was the voice of the moon. This scared the girls so much they screamed.

Sue remembers another time when Steven was baby-sitting her and her two sisters, and he stalked out of the bedroom with his face wrapped in toilet paper, looking like a mummy. Then he peeled the paper mask from his face layer by layer, and threw it at them.

Once he rigged a "bogeyman" in his closet to scare his sisters. He took a plastic skull that he bought at a model shop and put a light inside so the face glowed. Then he put his father's World War II aviator cap on the skull and goggles over the eyeholes.

That night Steven told his sisters that there was something in his closet. He dared them to go inside and investigate. They knew he was up to some trick. But, one by one, they slowly slid open the closet door and went inside. Then Steven plugged the extension cord into the wall, and the eyes on the skull lit up. The girls screamed. Eventually he let them out.

Although he enjoyed frightening his sisters, Steven wasn't the big, brave, older brother his sisters must have thought he was. He had his own "bogeyman" to contend with. "My biggest fear was a clown doll," he said. "And the tree I could see outside my room." He also thought things could be hiding under his bed, or in his closet.

16

Years later, Steven Spielberg wrote the ghost story for a movie called *Poltergeist*. A "poltergeist" is a "noisy ghost," which haunts a house by moving things around, but usually does not harm people. In Steven's story, the ghosts are bad. A tree crashes through a bedroom window at a young boy sleeping inside. A clown doll comes to life, and there is a whole closetful of nasty spirits.

TAKE TWO: Screen Testing

The first movie Steven Spielberg can remember seeing was about a traveling circus. The movie was called *The Greatest Show on Earth*, and Steven was about four and a half years old when he saw it. What he remembers the most from *The Greatest Show on Earth* was the train wreck sequence. To Steven, it seemed that the train jumped the tracks and landed in his lap. This excited his imagination. How was a movie was able to do this?

By the time the Spielbergs were living in Arizona,

Mr. Spielberg had a movie camera to film the family camping trips. Steven was always telling his father how to shoot the movies. One day, Arnold handed the camera over to Steven. "If you know so much, you try it," he told his son. And as soon as Steven had mastered the camera, he began making movies.

Steven filmed almost everything. One day he talked Mrs. Spielberg into letting a pot of cherries jubilee boil over on the stove so Steven could film the bubbly, sticky mess. When his mother asked Steven to film the family in their car, he took a movie of the hubcaps.

When he was twelve, Steven bought his own movie camera. The next year he enrolled in a Boy Scout photography class. For the class he made a three-minute movie about a cowboy who robbed a stagecoach; one of his friends played the cowboy. The finished project brought Steven his first award—a merit badge, and promotion to Eagle Scout.

The success of the Boy Scout photography class gave Steven more ideas. The family camping trips became movie sets. Steven would make his mother wait to open a can of beans until he had his camera set up. And he would call "Action" before he would let his dad clean a fish.

Steven began staging model train wrecks in his bedroom so that he could film them. He would put his eye right next to the tracks to see how his trains looked as they collided. Once he had figured out the angle he wanted to film, he would set up his movie camera, and stage the train wreck again.

"From age twelve or thirteen, I knew I wanted to be a movie director," Steven has said. But he didn't want to study in school. He couldn't see how classes like science, math or foreign languages were going to help him make movies. So while he was busy filming head-on train collisions, his class work suffered. Even though Steven now writes the screenplays for his movies, he is not a very fast reader. "And that is sort of a shame," he admits.

Instead of studying in class, Steven made little drawings in the margins of his textbooks. On page after page he would draw little figures, so when he flipped through the book, the images would move like a cartoon.

Steven didn't get along very well with his classmates either. Being small, he was often called a "nerd" by the other boys. He was called on last whenever the gang was choosing up sides for baseball, and he failed physical education class in high school three times.

He was also picked on by the "bullies" at his school. One of the worst bullies would knock Steven down on the lawn or hold his face in the water at the drinking fountain. Sometimes Steven even had to run home and hide in his room when the bully was looking for him.

Steven figured if you can't beat them, you can join them. So one day he asked the bully to star in a movie. At first the boy thought Steven was joking, but Steven convinced him that he needed the bigger kid to play a war hero in a movie called *Battle Squad*. Steven made him a squad leader in the movie, and the two became friends.

The ordeal of being picked on made a lasting impression on Steven. Years later, when Spielberg wrote the story for a movie called *Back to the Future*, he had one of the lead characters always being picked on by a group of tough kids.

By the time Steven was in high school, he had already made over fifteen short films, and the Phoenix *Gazette* had written a feature story about the young filmmaker. Yet he still felt like an outcast. It wasn't until he went to Phoenix's Arcadia High School and enrolled in the theater and arts program that he found other students with the same interests.

In the theater program there were other "nerds" who liked acting. "That's when I realized there were options besides being a jock or a wimp," he remembers.

The first full-length movie Steven made was a science fiction story he filmed when he was sixteen. The movie, called *Firelight*, was two and a half hours long—longer than most movies shown in movie theaters—and it cost $500 to make. Steven wrote the story, found the actors to play the parts (including his sister, Nancy), and put the film together in its finished form.

Every weekend for a year, Steven shot scenes for *Firelight*. On Monday he would fake illness so he could stay home and edit his film. He would put the thermometer up to a light bulb to heat it, so when his mother read it, it looked as if Steven had a fever. (This is the same trick Elliot does in the movie *E.T.*)

Steven says his mother caught on to his thermometer trick, but was so impressed with his film that she played along: Steven stayed home and worked on his movie. But his parents made him keep up with his homework by threatening to take away his film equipment if his grades fell.

Steven talked the manager of a Phoenix movie theater into showing *Firelight* for one evening. Today, Steven remembers that the movie was awful, but he managed to sell enough tickets to make back the money it cost to shoot the film. He even came away with a $100 profit. Steven has since lost the only copy of *Firelight*.

Shortly after *Firelight* was shown in the movie theater, the Spielbergs moved to California, and his mother and father separated. By this time Steven was sixteen, but the divorce of his parents affected him greatly. He later put those feelings into a movie. In *E.T.*, Elliot's parents are divorced, and the young hero feels left out of things because his father is not around.

Welcome to Hollywood

Steven moved a step closer to realizing his filmmaking dreams during the summer of 1965, when the seventeen-year-old movie buff toured Universal Studios in Los Angeles. The tour didn't satisfy Steven's curiosity because it didn't include visits to the sound stages, the areas where movie sets are built and the actual filming takes place. So, during a bathroom break, Steven snuck away from the tour group and wandered over to a sound stage. He watched the film crew for the rest of the day.

The next day, he wanted to return to the movie set. Without a pass, it can be difficult or even impossible to get into movie studios. Steven dressed in a business suit and carried a briefcase with his lunch in it. He looked official enough that the guard at the studio gate let him pass. For the rest of that summer, Steven went to the studio every day and hung around the movie sets, watching and asking questions.

When it was time for Steven to enroll in college, he knew he wanted to study movie-making. His grades weren't good enough to allow him into the University of California's excellent film school, or any of the other top California schools. Steven went to California State College in Long Beach.

He scheduled his classes so he would only have to be in school two days a week, and spent the rest of his time at Universal Studios. At Universal, Steven kept trying to get the studio bosses to look at the films he had made in high school. Those movies had been made on 8-millimeter (mm) film with no sound. One day, he was told that if he were to make movies with sound on 16-mm or 35-mm film, the sizes of film most commercial movies are made on, his movies would be seen by the top executives.

Encouraged, Steven set about making a movie on the larger film. Another student at Steven's college wanted to be a film producer, so he helped Steven raise the money for the better film and equipment. The young director wrote the script, and titled it *Amblin'*. A year later the project was finished.

The movie was about a boy and a girl hitchhiking from the desert to the Pacific Ocean. It was only twenty-three minutes long, but it showed that Spielberg knew how to handle the movie camera, understood lighting, and could direct actors.

In fact, *Amblin'* was good enough to impress the studio bosses at Universal. The day after Steven had shown them his film, they called and offered him a seven-year contract to direct television shows. Steven was twenty years old, and his dream of becoming a movie director was becoming reality. "I quit college so fast, I didn't even clean out my locker," he remembers.

The first show Steven directed for Universal was an episode of the television series "Night Gallery." The star of that episode was Joan Crawford, a legend in Hollywood who had been starring in movies since before Steven was born. Joan, like the bosses at Universal, was very impressed with the young director. When the show was finished, she said Steven was a genius.

After "Night Gallery," Steven went on to direct shows for the television series "Marcus Welby," "Columbo," and "Owen Marshall."

In 1971, Steven directed his first made-for-television movie, a thriller called *Duel*. In this picture, a mild-mannered man is driving a car across the United States. Along the way he is pursued and threatened by a large, black semi-trailer. Steven built suspense by never letting the audience see who is driving the truck.

Duel was so successful on American television that Universal decided to release it in the movie theaters in

Europe. There it became a big hit. Steven became even more anxious to make a film for the American movie theaters.

The idea for Steven's first major picture came from a newspaper clipping he had saved. It was a report of a Texas woman who hijacked a police car (with the police officer inside) and drove off to rescue her baby from an orphanage. The idea became *The Sugarland Express*, starring Goldie Hawn. The movie was only a minor box office success, but earned enough money to make the studios listen seriously to Spielberg's ideas.

The idea for Steven's next movie, about a shark attacking a seaside resort, came to him while he was finishing *The Sugarland Express*. During his free time, Spielberg had been reading the novel *Jaws*, and he thought the story would make a great picture. He was right: *Jaws* became the biggest box office hit of movie history.

There are a couple of reasons that *Jaws* was liked by so many people. First of all, the characters in the movie weren't super-heroes or famous people. They were simply ordinary people reacting to unusual situations. Also, Steven knew how to give the audience just enough details to keep them interested, and then move on to another part of the story. This layering technique builds the story a little bit of information at a time.

The next movie Steven made, *Close Encounters of the Third Kind*, used both of these techniques—ordinary people as the characters, and the layering of information. The movie is about visitors from outer space coming to

Richard Dreyfuss played the ordinary telephone repairman in *Close Encounters of the Third Kind.* **Here he is looking up at the blinding glare of light from the spaceship in his first encounter with the aliens.**

Earth, but the main character is an ordinary man who works for the telephone company. And Steven designed the movie so that the audience never really sees what the spaceship looks like until the last fifteen minutes of the movie. *Close Encounters* was another big hit for Steven Spielberg.

His next movie, however, didn't do as well at the box office. *1941* was a comedy set during World War II. It told how people in southern California reacted to a rumor that the Japanese were attacking the Los Angeles area. *1941* was so expensive to make—it included a scene in which a Ferris wheel falls off its stand and rolls into the ocean—that the movie made hardly any money.

The failure of *1941* didn't bother Spielberg much. By the time it came out, he was already working on his next picture, *Raiders of the Lost Ark*. This movie became even more popular than *Jaws* or *Close Encounters*. *Raiders* came from an idea of one of Steven's filmmaking friends, George Lucas.

Steven and George had known one another since 1967, when George was attending film school at the University of Southern California, a few miles north of Long Beach where Steven was studying. Like Steven, George Lucas had found tremendous success early in his career. One of George's first movies was *American Graffiti*, the story of a group of teenagers during their last night together before they all left for college. At the time, many people didn't believe that a movie about teenagers would appeal to audiences. But *American Graffiti* became the big hit of the summer of 1974. Lucas then went on to make *Star Wars*, the second most popular movie of all time.

Before *Star Wars* was to open in the movie theaters, and shortly after Spielberg had finished *Close Encounters*, the two young film directors took a vacation in Hawaii. There, on a beach, they built a huge sand castle for good luck, and began discussing projects they wanted to do. Steven said he had always wanted to do an adventure film, like the James Bond movies. George then told Steven his idea for a hero who isn't a secret agent, but an archeologist sent out by museums to recover lost treasures. Together, Spielberg and Lucas developed the story for *Raiders of the Lost Ark*.

After writing the screenplay, George turned the movie over to Steven to direct. Steven decided to re-create

Steven Spielberg with his Fellowship Award, the English equivalent of the Oscar, which he won in 1986.

the look of the adventure series he used to see in movie theaters when he was a child. The series were shown in ten- or fifteen-minute "chapters" before the main feature. At the end of each chapter, the hero (someone like Flash Gordon or the Lone Ranger) was in terrible danger. It would seem he was about to be run over by a train, or eaten by an alligator. The next

31

week, the new chapter would begin with the hero's amazing escape, and then go on to another adventure.

Raiders of the Lost Ark has the feel of those old series. The hero, Indiana Jones, saves himself from one difficult situation only to find himself in another. *Raiders*, released in 1981, put Steven back on his movie-making winning streak. He and George returned to Hawaii to build another sand castle and to celebrate. Spielberg's next project, however, broke all records, even his own.

In the summer of 1982, Steven released *E.T.* The story touched so many people, young and old, that it became the biggest-selling movie of all time.

That same summer, *Poltergeist* was released. Steven produced it, wrote the screenplay, and helped direct some of the scenes. The movie did very well at the theaters, and it helped to prove that Steven Spielberg knew what movie audiences wanted to see.

Steven wasn't about to slow down his movie-making. He started work with George Lucas on the second movie about Indiana Jones. *Indiana Jones and the Temple of Doom*, again directed by Steven, opened during the summer of 1984.

The same summer *Gremlins* opened at the movie theaters. This movie wasn't directed by Steven, although he did write the original story and helped produce it. Because he had been given the opportunity to direct movies when he was young, Steven had decided to help other young movie-makers get their start in the industry. *Gremlins* was his first project to do this.

In the summer of 1985, Steven again presented films which he wrote but did not direct. One of them, *Back to the Future*, became the big hit of the year. It is about a teenage boy who travels back in time and meets his parents before they are married. *Goonies* is the story of a group of kids who discover an old pirates' treasure in a cave along the Pacific coast.

Spielberg has said that his job in films such as *Gremlins, Back to the Future,* and *Goonies* was to make the young directors aware of their own best work, and to get them to do it.

Although he was helping other directors get their movies made, Spielberg had not stopped directing his own. During 1985, Steven directed *The Color Purple*. This was a little different from the other movies he had directed because it was not an adventure movie. It told the story of a black woman living in the South.

In 1985 Spielberg also returned to television. NBC began broadcasting "Amazing Stories," a series that was Steven's idea. Like a series of movies, the show had a new cast and told a new story every week. Of the first season's twenty-two shows, Steven wrote the stories for fifteen and directed four. "Amazing Stories" is one of the ways for all the ideas that Steven has to become more than just dreams.

Amblin Around

Even though Steven Spielberg is one of Hollywood's most successful movie directors, he says that his biggest and best production has been his son, Max Samuel Spielberg. His son was born in June of 1985. Steven's wife is Amy Irving, an actress Steven met in 1975.

Universal Studios, the movie company for which Spielberg has made most of his movies, has built a special office for him. The two-story adobe building has everything in it, from a forty-five-seat movie theater to a row of video games.

George Lucas and Steven Spielberg. The third movie in their Indiana Jones series is *The Further Adventure of Indiana Jones.*

Outside the building is a wooden bridge across a stream stocked with silver and gold Japanese fish called "koi." On these grounds Steven keeps his dog, a golden retriever named Brandy. The office complex is called Amblin, in honor of the twenty-three minute movie that helped the young movie-maker get his first job in Hollywood.

It doesn't look like the production schedule for the man Hollywood refers to as "Mr. Movies" will let up soon. After *The Color Purple*, Steven began work on the third chapter of the Indiana Jones stories. He says that Amblin, his production company, will make up to four movies a year. Steven will be the producer, and sometimes the screenwriter for these movies. Through these projects, Steven can continue to help young film-makers talent get the experience they need.

Steven has not retired from directing his own pictures. He hopes to direct a new picture every year and a half. "I don't think my parents ever figured movies would be something I'd succeed at," Steven has said. But there have been a lot of sand castles built on the beaches of Hawaii that have proven that idea wrong.

E.T. says goodbye to Elliott (Henry Thomas) before leaving Earth.

STEVEN SPIELBERG'S MOVIES

Listed by year of release. Steven's job in the making of each film is noted after the title.

1964   *Firelight.* Screenwriter, producer, director, cinematographer, editor. This was his first money-making film: he made $100.

1968   *Amblin'.* Director and screenwriter. This won him a prize at the 1969 Atlanta Film Festival and the job at Universal.

1971   *Duel* (for TV). Director.

1972   *Something Evil* (for TV). Director.
       Savage (for TV). Director.

1973   *The Sugarland Express.* Story development, director.
       Ace Eli and Rodger of the Skies. Story development.

1975   *Jaws.* Director. The fifth greatest money-making film of all time.*

1977   *Close Encounters of the Third Kind.* Director, screenwriter. The fourteenth greatest money-making film of all time.*

1978   *I Wanna Hold Your Hand.* Executive producer.

1979   *1941.* Director.

1981   *Raiders of the Lost Ark.* Director. The seventh greatest money-making film of all time.*

1982   *E.T.: The Extra-Terrestrial.* Producer, screenwriter, director. The most popular movie of all time.*
       Poltergeist. Producer, screenwriter.

1983   *Twilight Zone — The Movie.* Producer, co-director.

1984   *Indiana Jones and the Temple of Doom.* Director. The eighth greatest money-making film of all time.*
       Gremlins. Executive producer. The sixteenth greatest money-making film of all time.

1985   *Back to the Future.* Screenwriter, producer.
       Goonies. Screenwriter, producer.
       The Color Purple. Director, producer.

*From the 1985 list compiled by *Variety*.

39